CELEBRATE OUR LOVE
Couple's Journal

Name _____   Name _____

CELEBRATE OUR LOVE
Couple's Journal

120 Activities to Make Connecting Fun

Patrice Webb Bush

ROCKRIDGE
PRESS

Interior and Cover Designer: Julie Schrader
Interior Production Assistance: Patricia Fabricant
Art Manager: Janice Ackerman
Editor: Adrienne Ingrum
Production Editor: Kurt Shulenberger
Cover Maze Illustration: © 2019 Rightholder / istock.com; Cover Photo (Pencils): © 2019 Bennyartist/Shutterstock; Interior Stock Illustration: Under License from Shutterstock.com.

ISBN: Print 978-1-64152-966-2
R0

To my dear friend, mentor, and sister,
Ebony Moore, who lives in heaven:
Thank you for whispering in my ear
throughout this process. Your passion and
tenacity for "growth" live on through
everyone you taught to push through the
currents and keep swimming.

CONTENTS

INTRODUCTION

Congratulations on purchasing *Celebrate Our Love Couple's Journal: 125 Activities to Make Connecting Fun* to bring more spontaneity, fun, laughter, and romance into your relationship! Before I give you all the juicy details of this book, let me tell you a little bit about myself and why I wrote it.

I have been working to strengthen couples and families for more than thirteen years. As the founder and CEO of It Takes 2 Marriage Coaching, I have helped more than 650 couples across thirty-four states through my couples coaching, marriage retreats, workshops, and support groups. I also hosted the *Marriage Matters* radio show, which had more than 8,000 listeners.

One thing I've learned during my years of working with couples is the necessity of PLAY in adult relationships. It is very easy to get caught up in the everyday hustle-bustle of climbing the corporate ladder and tending to the kiddos, which leaves us little time to remember why or how we fell in love in the first place. I use lighthearted activities and games during my marriage retreats to get adults laughing and remind them how it feels to be a kid again. It is much easier to let down our guard and be vulnerable when we are having fun.

The activities in this book are designed to give you the opportunity to share all kinds of play—fun play, intimate play, intellectual play, experiential play, emotional play. Some activities will make you laugh until your stomach hurts, while others will make you cry tears of joy because you feel so close to your partner.

I have categorized each activity by a hashtag found at the top corner of each page:

#COMMUNICATION I'll introduce you to various forms of communication and help you figure out how best to bond with your partner so you both feel heard.

#COPARENTING These exercises will help you find balance as both parents and a couple so that everyone feels loved and connected.

#MONEYMATTERS Money is a major reason for discord in a relationship. This category will encourage deeper discussions about the topic to ensure you are both on the same page.

#PERSONALITYCOMPATIBILITY One gender is from Mars and the other Venus, right? Wrong! It's not about gender; it is about personality differences and how you process situations.

#IRS (Intimacy + Romance = Sex) You need a combination of intimacy and romance to keep your relationship fresh. These activities will certainly help.

#GETTINGALONG Learning how to successfully manage conflict will strengthen your relationship.

#DATENIGHT Sometimes you just want to enjoy your partner's company, and the exercises in this category will have you enjoying each other just like old times, even if you stay home.

Feel free to use the hashtags to focus on a specific topic you may be struggling with. Or, skip around. I recommend starting with a #DateNight activity or two. Opening up can be challenging, so let the playful competition of a few games or some dancing exercises help. When you are feeling more comfortable, jump right into the other categories and be sure to follow all directions and tips! You will notice some activities require you to set the mood with dim lights and candles, while others require some basic supplies. As a bonus, at the end of each exercise you will find "Reflections," which are journal prompts that encourage you to reflect on any new insights you gain about yourself or your partner as a result of the activity.

Finally, I would be remiss if I didn't mention the importance of playing fairly, honestly, and safely, both physically and emotionally. This book is meant to bring you closer. One partner sleeping on the couch while the other sleeps in the bed is not close, so play fair!

Have fun and remember: The couple that plays together, stays together!

First Date Memories

Paying attention to the details about your mate can make a big difference in a relationship. Below you will find questions about your first date. For each correct answer, you will receive a point. The person with more points will have dinner cooked and served to them over the next week by the person with fewer points.

Partner A

Where did your first date take place?

_____

What fragrance was your mate wearing?

_____

What fragrance were you wearing?

_____

What was the first thing you said to your mate?

_____

_____

_____

If there was food involved, what did you eat?

_____

What color was your mate wearing?

_____

What color did you wear?

Did the night end with a kiss?

Who asked whom out?

What surprised you the most about your mate?

What was your funniest memory of the date?

Partner B

Where did your first date take place?

What fragrance was your mate wearing?

What fragrance were you wearing?

What was the first thing you said to your mate?

If there was food involved, what did you eat?

What color was your mate wearing?

What color did you wear?

Did the night end with a kiss?

Who asked whom out?

_____

What surprised you the most about your mate?

_____

_____

What was your funniest memory of the date?

_____

_____

_____

Who owes whom dinner?

_____

REFLECTIONS What were your thoughts about your partner after your first date? Did you envision that you would be in a relationship?

Partner A

_____

_____

_____

Partner B

_____

_____

_____

A Couple Who Cooks Together . . .

. . . creates intimacy together! Pick a cuisine you haven't tried before and search online for a new dish. Buy the ingredients and prepare the meal together.

While cooking, play some soothing music, light a candle, and feel free to cook in as little or as much clothing as you like!

REFLECTIONS Do you feel closer as a result of cooking together? How many other cuisine options can you come up with to create in the future?

Partner A

Partner B

Compatibility Mix-Up

Find the personality terms inside this smiley face!

```
                    E Y V
                K E E L Y N J A Y
              T E A F V B G X Z Q K V S
            W I U M U W I A N M L A C F V C Y
          A F S B I Q L T E Q E I Z N D S O T E
        Q A X W V G S D A E Y A E G O L Y N R E L
        X G U G K G O Y R R N S L U X T B S E U S
      L H R L L F       E G Q Y A       E E V R U F
      A Z E A W X       P A A G I       T R O U E L
      J M J E I I Z B W M O S U O C N G W I V R I G S M
      S N S A C Y O A T J O I M I O Y T A Q A T J H I Q
      H I J B O D L J P I C D O N S G V R D T X R E W E
    C Q Y Z L S T X R P N F L C G I V V J O I E F U L M A
    C T N D E C I S I V E C S M H T U C T B V L U Y L H I
    K Q N F R C O M P A T I B L E N U Y O Y E E V M L U H
      B G E U   R F P A N E M Z Y A O S Z G H   R F H A
      B N D V     O Y I P O C C G L S J O O       Z T Q I
      Z W T B I     Y Y V U J N L Y O V L         R I E H O
      J R G A T                               Y C V A K
      I A P C G C                           S T I G S C
        Q T I E P A V G W L W E W R J T R S Y M O
        D O C I T S I T R A V W K M C Z S G Z U V
          Y P T V W E G Q A S S K E D E V W C S
            I F T X S L R B V J R A R V P W G
              N R X B P K J I F G A V R
                O Z Y M D A G B Q
                    Y O A
```

Term Clues

AGGRESSIVE	BRAVE	COOPERATIVE	EASYGOING
ANTISOCIAL	CALM	DECISIVE	EXTROVERT
ARTISTIC	COMPATIBLE	DIRECT	INTROVERT
BOSSY	CONSERVATIVE	DISAGREEABLE	SOCIAL

REFLECTIONS Do any of these terms describe you or your partner?

Partner A

Partner B

Hide & Get the Kisses

In this flirty twist on a childhood classic, one person slowly counts to twenty while the other partner hides. The partner who is hiding will leave a trail of Hershey's Kisses from the starting point to their hiding spot. Upon reaching twenty, the person counting will find their partner using the trail as a clue. Supplies needed: a bag of Hershey's Kisses or your favorite individually wrapped candy.

TIP: Play this until you finish the bag of Kisses! ;-) More Kisses equals more kisses!

REFLECTIONS Did the game increase your relationship's intimacy?

Partner A

Partner B

Dance Party!

Select a song and then retreat to separate rooms for twenty minutes to create a new dance. Come back and teach each other your new dances. Combine them into a routine and dance to your hearts' content during the song you selected at the beginning. Supplies needed: a computer, smartphone, or other device that plays music.

REFLECTIONS Write one word to describe how it felt to create something with your partner.

Partner A

_____

Partner B

_____

I Can Show You the World

The United States isn't the world, but it is vast and diverse. In this exercise, each partner will use a different color marker and take turns circling the states they have visited. Supplies needed: two markers of different colors.

Alabama	Hawaii	Massachusetts	New Mexico	South Dakota
Alaska	Idaho	Michigan	New York	Tennessee
Arizona	Illinois	Minnesota	North Carolina	Texas
Arkansas	Indiana	Mississippi	North Dakota	Utah
California	Iowa	Missouri	Ohio	Vermont
Colorado	Kansas	Montana	Oklahoma	Virginia
Connecticut	Kentucky	Nebraska	Oregon	Washington
Delaware	Louisiana	Nevada	Pennsylvania	West Virginia
Florida	Maine	New Hampshire	Rhode Island	Wisconsin
Georgia	Maryland	New Jersey	South Carolina	Wyoming

REFLECTIONS Which states would you like to visit together? Set a goal for a vacation and make it happen!

Partner A

Partner B

Let's Get Through It!

If you work together, you can get through anything! Together, unscramble the conflict resolution–related words below.

1. iamensteeDrg
2. eevsoRl
3. tGrhwo
4. nitasDt
5. eteegmArn
6. ehpztaEmi
7. nlCfcoti
8. giaTnkl
9. elginlY
10. oCep
11. eExrolp
12. evLo
13. rreTiggs
14. emrmCsiopo
15. rgoenI
16. ncptePoeri
17. iooEtnsm
18. oiuRleston
19. lpvEisxoe
20. nLitngise

REFLECTIONS Did any of these terms resonate with you?

Partner A

Partner B

Time of Day

Think about your partner's personality. The numbers below correspond to a specific time of day. Answer each question about your partner by putting the corresponding number on the line.

1. Morning
2. Afternoon
3. Evening

What time of day is your partner . . .

Most annoying?   Partner A _____   Partner B _____

Most silly?   Partner A _____   Partner B _____

Most grumpy?   Partner A _____   Partner B _____

Most productive?   Partner A _____   Partner B _____

Most sociable?   Partner A _____   Partner B _____

Most quiet?   Partner A _____   Partner B _____

Most distracted?   Partner A _____   Partner B _____

Most talkative?   Partner A _____   Partner B _____

Most playful?   Partner A _____   Partner B _____

Most touchy?   Partner A _____   Partner B _____

Most serious?   Partner A _____   Partner B _____

Most hungry?   Partner A _____   Partner B _____

Most flirty?   Partner A _____   Partner B _____

REFLECTIONS Do you take advantage of the times of the day when your partner is most positive? Do you find yourself avoiding them when they are most negative?

Partner A

Partner B

Ah-Mazing Fun!

Ready, set, go! Who can complete the maze faster? Time each other and enjoy!

Partner A

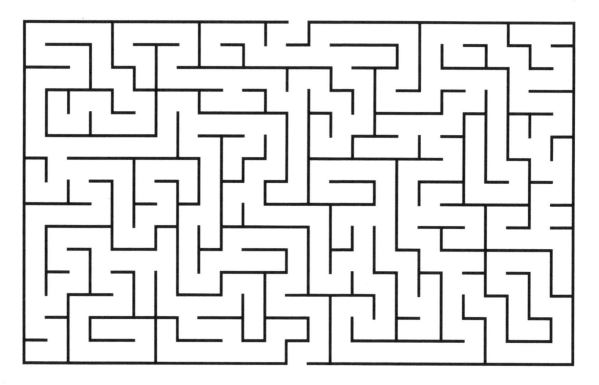

Partner B

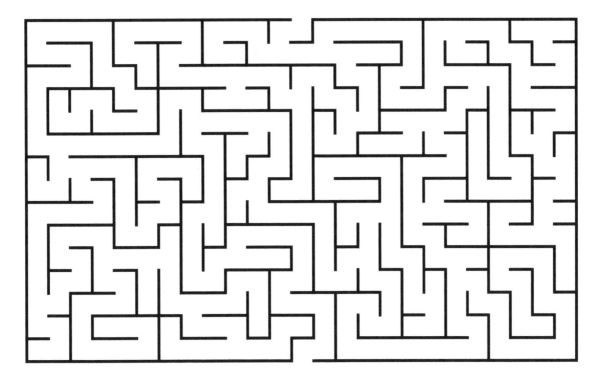

REFLECTIONS Who was faster? How did it feel to complete this exercise?

Partner A

_____

_____

Partner B

_____

_____

Dice Up Some Intimacy!

In this exercise, you'll have to find creative ways to foster intimacy with your partner. Roll the dice. If you roll an even number, you must use nonverbal intimacy, meaning no speaking! Use your senses, such as touch, taste, smell, and sight. Remember: no talking!

If you roll an odd number, then you must use verbal intimacy. Use your words to flirt with each other. Supplies needed: a pair of dice.

REFLECTIONS Which was easier: verbal or nonverbal intimacy?

Partner A

_____

_____

Partner B

_____

_____

Are You That Parent?

Each partner will answer the True/False questions below and then discuss their views of parenting.

Partner A	True	False
I tell my kids I love them every day.	☐	☐
I hug and kiss my children daily.	☐	☐
I encourage my kids to follow their dreams.	☐	☐
I cook for my kids at least four times a week.	☐	☐
My kids eat takeout or at a restaurant at least four times a week.	☐	☐
I allow my kids to pick out their own clothes.	☐	☐
I treat all of my children equally.	☐	☐
My kids sleep in their own beds.	☐	☐
We take family trips.	☐	☐
I allow my partner to discipline our children.	☐	☐
I allow my children to spend the night with their peers.	☐	☐
I apologize to my children when I am wrong.	☐	☐
I want to be my children's friend more than I want to be their parent.	☐	☐
I know my children's goals and dreams.	☐	☐
My children know my goals and dreams.	☐	☐
My children and I have created traditions together.	☐	☐
My partner and I agree on how to raise our children.	☐	☐

Partner B	True	False
I tell my kids I love them every day.	☐	☐
I hug and kiss my children daily.	☐	☐
I encourage my kids to follow their dreams.	☐	☐
I cook for my kids at least four times a week.	☐	☐
My kids eat takeout or at a restaurant at least four times a week.	☐	☐
I allow my kids to pick out their own clothes.	☐	☐
I treat all of my children equally.	☐	☐
My kids sleep in their own beds.	☐	☐
We take family trips.	☐	☐
I allow my partner to discipline our children.	☐	☐
I allow my children to spend the night with their peers.	☐	☐
I apologize to my children when I am wrong.	☐	☐
I want to be my children's friend more than I want to be their parent.	☐	☐
I know my children's goals and dreams.	☐	☐
My children know my goals and dreams.	☐	☐
My children and I have created traditions together.	☐	☐
My partner and I agree on how to raise our children.	☐	☐

REFLECTIONS Are there areas of parenting that you want to improve?

Partner A

Partner B

Artistic Antics

Flip a coin to determine who starts. The first person begins by drawing a line, circle, or other item and then you take turns adding onto the picture. Set a predetermined number of turns, and when you have reached that number, admire the masterpiece you both created! Supplies needed: a fairly large piece of paper; colored pencils, crayons, or markers.

REFLECTIONS Did your drawing surprise you? How good are you at working together and compromising?

Partner A

_____

_____

_____

Partner B

_____

_____

_____

Backside Conversation

Communication is the foundation of all relationships. Your communication with your mate will either take your relationship to the next level or keep it stagnant.

Partner A, sit on the floor behind Partner B, giving yourself full access to their back. Think of a series of things—for example: shapes, symbols, words, or phrases—and draw one on your partner's back with your finger. You cannot speak. Partner B, figure out what Partner A drew. After four rounds, switch positions.

> **REFLECTIONS** Was that activity easy or difficult? What are some challenges that come along with communication? Is it difficult to communicate without words? Have you ever been limited in your communication? Have you been successful in communicating without using words in the past?

Partner A

_____

_____

_____

Partner B

_____

_____

_____

Kiss 'n' Tell

Work together to find intimacy-related words in this sexy word search.

```
        E I D E M                          Y P U W L
        J I P T Q J T                    O L S W T D Z
      G N A O M M K V X S            P R E E C L A N L T
    B M J C L C G D K Y U H        F Q A O K O X I Q K W H
    S L I J V A W N K L Z E G    S V S F A U B A U O R R B
  B S S K C R N A P I W I U P K A B U V I O G D X T O W O C R
  U K C I L Y D P N P D H S X K A R K N T A R L L S B V B L P
  A L B X K M L G D S S L P D I E A T D R K T E O Z R K Q C G
  E F P H M X E S O D R M O U Y C I J N S O A C P V W N D X G
  E D Z N X R J A O N A N P H D M L Z J X F A A N L E A N I X
  V Y Z A I H B Y S A Q M S M A W M C N O I N T I M A C Y R H
  I F D E I Y E R P H R S Y T D K Q D P L H L U B P B Y V H T
  C T H O N G I T B I E P E D P L U V K L V T O T G Z U P C S
    F S G A J T U I R X E K Q I M Z W W M N A S B O X E R S
  W G X V Y I W A T T N H Y M O S B Z I Y F K W E Q L L D
    R S B V T C L D T L P N F W T C X D U S N G M Y E H
      I Q X H X V O P A E F P P B E P Y C I A F E I Q
        B I M I D G Y B S J F R T Y A L O S P M M J
        G Z O S E X X B O K P O M D C S B E R O
          U Z B Z I L E T I R E C N A M O R Q
          F W Q N K N S O Q Z J M M W Y N
            C F H W M Q V S N U E U O A
            C H F D R V U M E D V B
              S U F V R S G M J Q
              W C E K Y G A S
              U H C U O T
              M Z F D
              Y F
```

Word Search Clues

BOXERS	HANDS	KISS	MASSAGE	SEXY
CANDLE	HOLDING	LICK	MOAN	SILK
CARESS	HUG	LINGERIE	OILS	THONG
FOREPLAY	INTIMATE	LOVE	PLEASURE	TOUCH

REFLECTIONS Are you going to add anything from these clues to your love life?

Partner A

Partner B

Can You Stand to Sing?

One partner says a song title and the other must sing a verse of that song. For every verse the partner sings correctly, they earn a point.

Partner A Songs
(feel free to substitute):

1. "Live Your Life"—T.I.
2. "Boulevard of Broken Dreams"—Green Day
3. "I Kissed a Girl"—Katy Perry
4. "SexyBack"—Justin Timberlake
5. "Speechless"—Dan + Shay
6. "Bootylicious"—Destiny's Child
7. "Jesus, Take the Wheel"— Carrie Underwood
8. "Forever and for Always"— Shania Twain

Partner B Songs
(feel free to substitute):

1. "We Belong Together"— Mariah Carey
2. "Get the Party Started"—Pink
3. "Since U Been Gone"— Kelly Clarkson
4. "In da Club"—50 Cent
5. "This Love"—Maroon 5
6. "I Will Always Love You"— Whitney Houston
7. "It's Gonna Be Me"—N'Sync
8. "Beautiful Day"—U2

REFLECTIONS Are you afraid to sing out loud? Did you have fun trying?

Partner A

Partner B

Relate, Resolve, Release

Copy the three words below onto pieces of paper, then fold them up and put them inside a bowl. Take turns drawing one out of the bowl and share with your partner a time in your relationship when you have had to relate, resolve, or release.

RELATE—This means "to make a connection." If you can relate to someone's story, something similar has happened to you.

RESOLVE—This means "to loosen, undo, or settle." You have found a solution to a problem or conflict. It has been "undone," so to speak.

RELEASE—This means letting go of a strong emotion such as anger, fear, anxiety, or frustration, especially as it relates to your relationship with your mate.

REFLECTIONS Was it helpful to share those situations with your partner? Did they agree with your assessment?

Partner A

Partner B

Words in Pairs

Directions: Using only two words, describe your partner's . . .

Partner A's answers about Partner B

CATEGORIES	DESCRIPTIVE WORDS
Personality	
Feet	
Smile	
Hands	
Hair	
Sleeping habits	
Cooking	
Driving	
Eyes	
Body	
Reading skills	
Nails	
Fashion sense	
Smell	
Laugh	

Partner B's answers about Partner A

CATEGORIES	DESCRIPTIVE WORDS
Personality	
Feet	
Smile	
Hands	
Hair	
Sleeping habits	
Cooking	
Driving	
Eyes	
Body	
Reading skills	
Nails	
Fashion sense	
Smell	
Laugh	

REFLECTIONS Were you surprised by any words your partner used? What was your favorite description?

Partner A

Partner B

Act It Out!

Dust off your acting skills and have fun with your partner! Write various categories on slips of paper, pull one, and take turns acting out something related to that subject. Your partner will try to guess what you are doing. Remember: Don't use any words!

Supplies needed: notepad, pencil for keeping score, slips of paper for the categories.

Suggested categories

- » **Books**
- » **Movies**
- » **Phrases**
- » **Plays**
- » **Songs**
- » **Television Shows**

Scores

Partner A _____   **Partner B** _____

REFLECTIONS Is one of you the better actor? The better guesser? How did this game make you feel?

Partner A
_____
_____
_____

Partner B
_____
_____
_____

Babies 'n' Things

Complete the crossword puzzle below. Use the lighthearted clues as you laugh about the joys of parenthood.

Puzzle Words

BABYSITTER	NURSING	CURIOUS	STROLLER	CUDDLE
DOCTORS	LOVE	KISSES	SLEEPY	VOMIT
POOP	CRY	SILLY	PLAY	TOYS

Across

6. At the beginning, your baby will see them often, and after a while, your baby will only see them annually.

8. What your child does when they want your attention, or are hungry, sleepy, sick, and everything in between.

9. After being up with a newborn for seven consecutive nights, you feel . . .

11. After every meal, put your nose plug on and grab your gloves because there is bound to be some.

12. Rattle, stuffed animals, bears, blocks.

13. Sometimes it has two wheels or four wheels, and it is a lifesaver in public.

15. Your lips just can't help it! You probably plant these on your little one daily.

Down

1. What a baby does after you give them a bottle and then attempt to play with them.

2. Your favorite thing to do with your new little bundle of joy.

3. An intimate connection between Mommy and baby.

4. They may be a teenager, but they love your children as their own.

5. There is nothing sweeter than coming home from work and getting to be _____ with your child(ren).

7. Children love to explore and are _____ about the world.

10. What children want to do as soon as your eyes close for a nap.

14. What we feel for our children the second they are born.

REFLECTIONS What surprised you about completing this exercise?

Partner A

Partner B

Coloring to Relax

More and more often, adults are discovering just how relaxing coloring can be, so pull out a box of crayons and release your inner kindergartner! Have fun with these images!

REFLECTIONS Did you find this exercise relaxing? Do you think you will color together more often?

Partner A

Partner B

Tic-Tac-Toe

Grab a pen or pencil and enjoy some old-fashioned competition! Keep track of the score and create a prize for the winner!

Scores

Partner A _____   Partner B _____

REFLECTIONS Did you want to help your partner? Did you see strategies that your partner didn't use?

Partner A   Partner B

_____   _____

_____   _____

_____   _____

Match Up Your Resolution

Work together to match the words on the left side of the page with the definitions on the right side by putting the corresponding letter on the line.

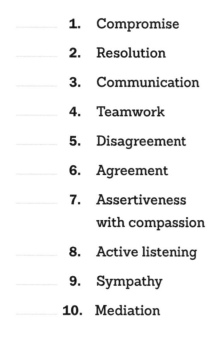

1. Compromise
2. Resolution
3. Communication
4. Teamwork
5. Disagreement
6. Agreement
7. Assertiveness with compassion
8. Active listening
9. Sympathy
10. Mediation

a) Life is easier when you have someone on your side, so choose to be on your partner's team, and you will see results in your relationship.

b) Each partner will have to meet in the middle to allow the relationship to win.

c) Being assertive is a necessary skill for the longevity of your relationship. You must be honest and upfront with your feelings but wrap your words in compassion so that your partner can receive them.

d) It is important to understand your partner's feelings, actions, or situation.

e) Conflict is a part of most relationships and can be a significant source of stress. Sweeping things under the rug will just cause the conflict to reappear, so it's important to deal with it.

f) The ability to fully concentrate on what is being said.

g) Having the same or similar views as your partner.

h) A process for resolving disputes in which an impartial party, such as a relationship counselor or clergy member, helps negotiate a solution.

i) When you and your partner have opposing views.

j) An exchange between partners that expresses honesty in assertion and listening.

REFLECTIONS Which items in this exercise were easiest?

Partner A

Partner B

Can You See It?

Communication can help a situation become either clearer or more distorted. In this exercise, Partner A will draw a picture. It can be anything, but make sure to keep the image secret from your partner. Then Partner A will describe it to Partner B. Partner B has to draw what they are hearing. When finished, see how close Partner B gets to the original picture drawn by Partner A. Then switch roles and give the other partner a chance!

    This is not an art contest. It's a communication partnership. Communicating clearly will help your partner draw the closest duplicate of your picture. Ready, set, go!

Supplies needed: paper; pens or pencils.

REFLECTIONS In your relationship, there will be times when one partner will have to trust the other even if you can't "see" their vision. How difficult is it to visualize something that you can't see?

Partner A

Partner B

How Deep Is Your Love?

Write down between five and ten relationship categories across the top of a piece of paper. Some suggestions are:

- » Love Songs
- » Honeymoon Location
- » Perfumes/Cologne
- » Terms of Endearment
- » Romantic Comedies

- » Sensual Scents
- » Flirty Fashions
- » Anniversary Gifts
- » Date Night Spots
- » Tempting Desserts

One partner chooses any random letter of the alphabet, and the other has two minutes to write as many words for each category that begin with that letter as they can. Make sure you keep score. The more obscure the words, the more fun!

REFLECTIONS How does it feel to make decisions under pressure? How will you and your partner make decisions in intense situations?

Partner A

Partner B

Taste the Rainbow

Take turns tasting different foods while blindfolded. Every time your partner correctly identifies a food, give them a point. (Please be aware of any food allergies that your partner may have and, of course, use only edible items.)

Supplies needed: blindfold, food.

Here are some food ideas to get started with!

» Fruit	» Crushed ice	» Pie
» Candy	» Cookies	» Bread
» Syrup	» Cheese	» Cereal
» Whipped cream	» Crackers	
» Ice cream	» Cake	

Scores

Partner A _____   **Partner B** _____

REFLECTIONS Does the taste of a food change if you can't see it?

Partner A

_____

_____

_____

Partner B

_____

_____

_____

Blockbuster Love

Imagine that Steven Spielberg is sitting at your dinner table. This could be your BIG break! Pitch a movie about your love story complete with a title, tagline, description, and characters. Get creative! Which celebrities would you and your partner cast as yourselves?

REFLECTIONS What do you think others would learn from your story?

Partner A

Partner B

Cookie Cook-Off

It's time for a cookie cook-off! Can't cook? No worries! Go to the grocery store and grab a pack of frozen cookie dough and toppings that will pair well with the cookies. Get in the kitchen and bake your cookies together. Once they are finished, add your toppings and serve each other your creations. Vote on who made the best cookie. Add some romance to the cook-off by playing slow music, dimming the lights, and cooking by candlelight, and kissing and touching each other as you feed each other bites of cookie. Supplies needed: frozen cookie dough, assorted cookie toppings (e.g., icing, whipped cream, sprinkles, edible glitter, chocolate chips).

Best Cookie Award goes to _____!

REFLECTIONS Did you consider your partner's taste buds to help you win the bake-off?

Partner A

_____

_____

Partner B

_____

_____

Band of Sounds

Get ready to listen! Gather several items from around the house that produce some sort of sound. Blindfold your partner and have them guess the item from the sound it makes. Get creative and have fun! Supplies needed: random things from around the house, blindfold. Some suggestions:

- » A stapler—staple a paper
- » A glass—hit the side with a spoon
- » A pill bottle—shake it
- » A piece of paper—tear it
- » A comb—rub your fingers along the teeth

- » Wood blocks—bang them together
- » A pot with a lid—place the lid on top noisily
- » Bottle of soda—open it
- » Door—close it

REFLECTIONS How good of a listener are you? Has your partner ever told you that you were not listening? How can you improve your listening skills?

Partner A

Partner B

Unplug to Plug In

Here's a fun fact: The average American spends close to ten hours a day on their phone, according to a recent Nielsen Company report. Between work emails, constant social media notifications, and taking selfies, it's easy to see how you can get caught up in screen time. However, being glued to your phones does not promote healthy quality time. When both of you set the screen to black, it promotes bonding. Each day, set some time aside for you both to turn off your phones completely and focus on each other.

Ask yourselves the following:

QUESTION	PARTNER A	PARTNER B
What is an appropriate length of time to turn off our phones?		
How often can we commit to unplugging?		
What types of things will we do when we unplug?		
What are our apprehensions about unplugging?		
What are the benefits to unplugging?		

REFLECTIONS Disconnecting from our phones can feel like a sacrifice. Are you game to make that sacrifice and benefit from truly connecting?

Partner A

Partner B

Cootie Combination

Ready, set, draw! The object of this game is to be the first to draw a completed cootie bug. Roll the die, and the person with the higher roll goes first. The number of dots on the die represents a different body part to draw, but first you must roll a one for the body and a two for the head. After you get the body and head, cootie parts can be added in any order. However, if you roll a number of a cootie part that you already have, your turn is over. Be creative with your cootie and make it uniquely yours!

Supplies needed: paper, pens, one die.

1 = body
2 = head
3 = antennae, hat, or bow

4 = eye
5 = tongue, teeth, or lips
6 = leg

REFLECTIONS Which aspect of your partner's drawing is the silliest?

Partner A

Partner B

Have a Bowling "Ball"!

Collect ten empty plastic water bottles and then fill them partially with water for stability. Arrange them in a bowling pin formation and use the ball to knock down the pins. Decide how many "frames" you are going to bowl and give out one point for each pin that gets knocked down. Winner receives a massage!

Supplies needed: ten empty same-size plastic water bottles, water, medium-size ball.

Scores

Partner A _____   Partner B _____

REFLECTIONS What things are not working with your communication that you need to knock down?

Partner A

_____

_____

_____

Partner B

_____

_____

_____

Enough Time in the Day

Think about how much time your partner spends on the items below and fill out the grid accordingly. Afterward, grade each other on your accuracy!

PARTNER A ON PARTNER B	UNDER 1 HOUR	1–2 HOURS	2–3 HOURS	3–5 HOURS	BULK OF DAY	NO TIME
Scrolling through social media						
Watching TV						
Playing video games						
Playing games on phone						
Working						
Shopping						
Romance						
Cleaning						
Self-care						
Drinking adult beverages						

PARTNER B ON PARTNER A	UNDER 1 HOUR	1–2 HOURS	2–3 HOURS	3–5 HOURS	BULK OF DAY	NO TIME
Scrolling through social media						
Watching TV						
Playing video games						
Playing games on phone						
Working						
Shopping						
Romance						
Cleaning						
Self-care						
Drinking adult beverages						

REFLECTIONS How accurate do you feel your partner was on the use of their time?

Partner A

Partner B

REFLECTIONS Do you wish your partner spent more or less time doing certain things?

Partner A

Partner B

Building a Future

Sometimes it's the small things that bring us together. Use toothpicks and mini marshmallows to design your future home.

Supplies needed: toothpicks, mini marshmallows.

REFLECTIONS How did it feel to talk about your future home?

Partner A

Partner B

Money Management Is King!

Money can be a hot topic in relationships, but if you talk about it in advance, it doesn't have to cause anxiety! As you unscramble the words below, discuss them and how they apply to your relationship.

1. ignninfac
2. ahsc
3. niceom
4. rsi
5. retdic
6. nile
7. tssea
8. lctaaip
9. noal
10. ecefarticit fo sopdiet
11. ari
12. eepesxns
13. aduti
14. bedt
15. onaccut

16. uebdtg   _____

17. dnob   _____

18. sach dvneaac   _____

19. ilne fo iretcd   _____

20. etla eef   _____

21. ddeidniv   _____

22. entsnteivms   _____

23. yemon   _____

24. sasvgin   _____

25. kcotss   _____

26. rmrteiente   _____

27. galso   _____

REFLECTIONS Did you learn anything new about your partner's philosophy about money? What are some similarities and differences you have on this topic?

Partner A

_____

_____

_____

Partner B

_____

_____

_____

Gifted Children

Spending money on gifts for your kids is good, but sometimes the personal touch is best. Instead of buying a gift for your kids, what if you and your partner worked together to make them a gift? Get creative and have fun! Supplies needed: Use your imagination. Here are some suggestions to get you started: paint, coloring tools, a small box, newspaper, magazines, glue, glitter, a mason jar.

REFLECTIONS What did you create? Was it easy to combine both of your ideas into one?

Partner A

Partner B

If This World Were Mine

At some point in all of our lives, someone has said to us, "This world does not revolve around you!" Well, let's pretend for a moment that the world DOES revolve around you! How would your world operate? Take turns going through the list.

If I had my own perfume, it would be called . . .
If I had my dream job, it would be . . .
If my best friend were a celebrity, they would be . . .
If I were the president, the first executive order I would make is . . .
If I could have any animal as a pet, it would be . . .
If I could drive any car, it would be . . .
If I could live anyplace in the world, it would be . . .
If I had to choose between money and fame, it would be . . .
If money were no object, I would buy . . .
If I were a singer, my stage name would be . . .
If I had a theme song, it would be . . .

REFLECTIONS What did you learn about your mate?

Partner A

Partner B

Change the Game!

When you change individually, the relationship itself can't help but follow suit. Use each section to process where your relationship is today and where you want to be going forward.

Limiting beliefs that you need to release:

Partner A: _____

Partner B: _____

Favorite relationship memory:

Partner A: _____

Partner B: _____

Intentions for the upcoming year:

Partner A: _____

Partner B: _____

Changes for Partner A

_____

_____

_____

Changes for Partner B

_____

_____

_____

REFLECTIONS What type of changes do you need to make individually? What type of collective changes would make your relationship better?

Partner A

_____

_____

Partner B

_____

_____

And the Oscar Goes to . . .

Movies are a great way to travel to different places and experience life vicariously. Two people can watch the same movie yet come away with different opinions about it. Discuss the categories below with your partner and see how much you agree . . . or not.

Favorite Comedy:

Favorite Horror Movie:

Favorite Romance:

Favorite Action Movie:

Favorite Thriller:

Favorite Actress:

Favorite Actor:

_____   _____

Movie That Changed the World:

_____   _____

Movie That Changed You:

_____   _____

Movie That You Wish You Starred in:

_____   _____

REFLECTIONS Is there a movie that has special significance for you and your partner?

Partner A   Partner B

_____   _____

_____   _____

Circle Gets the Square

When it comes to intimacy in a relationship, you have to keep it spicy. In each of the squares below, you and your partner should draw an image that represents something that gets the other in the mood. Then write a sentence that describes how you both can use this to your advantage!

Partner A

Partner B

REFLECTIONS How are you going to use the image to help your partner get in the mood?

Partner A

Partner B

When Was the Last Time?

Answer these questions about each other and see if you remember the last time your honey made you feel special!

Partner A

When was the last time your partner fixed you a meal?

When was the last time your partner surprised you?

When was the last time your partner planned a date?

When was the last time your partner let you choose a movie to watch together?

When was the last time your partner gave you a massage?

When was the last time your partner took the kids somewhere without you?

When was the last time your partner sacrificed for your family?

When was the last time your partner ran you a bath?

When was the last time your partner brought you a sweet treat?

When was the last time your partner brought you an item of clothing?

When was the last time your partner fixed your plate?

When was the last time your partner made you laugh?

When was the last time your partner made you cry?

When was the last time your partner confessed their love for you?

When was the last time you and your partner did something adventurous?

Partner B

When was the last time your partner fixed you a meal?

_____

When was the last time your partner surprised you?

_____

When was the last time your partner planned a date?

_____

When was the last time your partner let you choose a movie to watch together?

_____

When was the last time your partner gave you a massage?

_____

When was the last time your partner took the kids without you?

_____

When was the last time your partner sacrificed for your family?

_____

When was the last time your partner ran you a bath?

_____

When was the last time your partner brought you a sweet treat?

_____

When was the last time your partner brought you an item of clothing?

_____

When was the last time your partner fixed your plate?

_____

When was the last time your partner made you laugh?

_____

When was the last time your partner made you cry?

_____

When was the last time your partner confessed their love for you?

_____

When was the last time you and your partner did something adventurous?

_____

REFLECTIONS Were you embarrassed by some of the answers? How can you do a better job of making your partner feel special?

Partner A

_____

_____

Partner B

_____

_____

Enjoy the Silence

When you see a couple sitting quietly together and not talking, it is easy to assume that they must not be getting along. However, silence is not bad. It's actually a form of communication. If we listen closely, we can pick up on what is being UNsaid.

Turn off all sounds and distractions, including phones and televisions. Make sure you are touching in some way; you can lie in each other's arms, hold hands, or slow-dance (without music). Challenge yourselves to be quiet for twenty minutes. Then take your time and ease into conversation. Tell each other what you were thinking during the silence.

REFLECTIONS How easy was it to be silent? How did it feel to do this exercise with your mate?

Partner A

Partner B

Chip off the Ol' Block

Partner A: Describe your ideal relationship with your parents. Now describe your ideal relationship with your own children. Where are the correlations between these two types of relationships? Are you the parent you want to be?

REFLECTIONS What type of parent are you? Are you more like YOUR parents than you thought?

Partner A

Partner B: Describe your ideal relationship with your parents. Now describe your ideal relationship with your own children. Where are the correlations between these two types of relationships? Are you the parent you want to be?

REFLECTIONS What type of parent are you? Are you more like YOUR parents than you thought?

Partner B

You Are So Predictable!

When you have known someone for a while, you learn their mannerisms and quirks. Let's put your knowledge of your partner to the test! Think about your partner's behaviors and answer the following questions:

Partner A

1. Your partner plans a surprise for your birthday. It is . . .

a) A perfectly organized day doing what you love
b) A romantic date with a few mishaps but tons of fun
c) Dinner at a favorite restaurant that you both like and frequent
d) A date doing something THEY love more than you like

2. You buy your partner a present that they don't like. Do they . . .

a) Pretend to love it and use it anyway so they don't hurt your feelings
b) Tell the truth and ask to return it
c) Sell it online without telling you and use the money for something they really want
d) Start an argument with you about it and whine until you buy them something else

3. You tell your partner an embarrassing secret about yourself. Do they . . .

a) Take it to their grave
b) Tell only their best friend, who promises not to repeat it
c) Blurt it out in front of others to get a laugh
d) Post about it on social media because it's too juicy to keep to themselves

4. **You and your partner are out to dinner and your partner sees their ex. Do they . . .**

a) Pretend that they don't see them and avoid them
b) Introduce the ex as a family friend when the ex walks over
c) Introduce the ex honestly as their ex when the ex walks over
d) Walk over to the ex and speak to catch up on what they have missed in their life

5. **It is a family holiday and extended family is at your home. Your mother-in-law begins to joke about your housekeeping. Does your partner . . .**

a) Defend you immediately
b) Join in the joke with their mother and let you know that you don't clean like their mother
c) Sit quietly because, after all, she's their mom and she is always right
d) Put everyone out of the house and comfort you to ensure you feel emotionally safe

Partner B

1. Your partner plans a surprise for your birthday. It is . . .

a) A perfectly organized day doing what you love
b) A romantic date with a few mishaps but tons of fun
c) Dinner at a favorite restaurant that you both like and frequent
d) A date doing something THEY love more than you like

2. You buy your partner a present that they don't like. Do they . . .

a) Pretend to love it and use it anyway so they don't hurt your feelings
b) Tell the truth and ask to return it
c) Sell it online without telling you and use the money for something they really want
d) Start an argument with you about it and whine until you buy them something else

3. You tell your partner an embarrassing secret about yourself. Do they . . .

a) Take it to their grave
b) Tell only their best friend, who promises not to repeat it
c) Blurt it out in front of others to get a laugh
d) Post about it on social media because it's too juicy to keep to themselves

4. You and your partner are out to dinner and your partner sees their ex. Do they . . .

a) Pretend that they don't see them and avoid them
b) Introduce the ex as a family friend when the ex walks over

c) Introduce the ex honestly as their ex when the ex walks over

d) Walk over to the ex and speak to catch up on what they have missed in their life

5. It is a family holiday and extended family is at your home. Your mother-in-law begins to joke about your housekeeping. Does your partner . . .

a) Defend you immediately

b) Join in the joke with their mother and let you know that you don't clean like their mother

c) Sit quietly because, after all, she's their mom and she is always right

d) Put everyone out of the house and comfort you to ensure you feel emotionally safe

REFLECTIONS Was it challenging to guess how your partner would respond?

Partner A

Partner B

CEO Mindset

You and your partner are starting a business together. Collaborate on a business plan and decide the financial aspects of your new company.

Name of the company:

_____

Mission statement:

_____

_____

_____

Competitors:

_____

_____

_____

How will you get the start-up money?

_____

_____

What are your six-month to one-year financial goals?

_____

_____

_____

What is your five-year plan?

What are the challenges you may face?

REFLECTIONS Could you work with your partner?

Partner A

Partner B

Work-Life Balance

People who are able to balance their priorities have the most successful relationships. How do you keep yourself balanced? Think about the percentage of time you spend daily involved in each of these activities and then write it on the line.

ACTIVITY	PARTNER A	PARTNER B
Work		
Time together as a couple		
Family time		
Individual alone time		
Individual time with other friends		
Individual time with other family		

REFLECTIONS As you look over how you spend your time, what needs to change to have a more balanced life?

Partner A

Partner B

Walk with Me

Quality time is not only an important way to get to know your partner, it is also a way to build intimacy. The more quality time you spend with your partner, the more chances for intimacy. How would you respond in the following scenario?

You are going to the store to grab a few things for your household. As you walk out the door, your partner says, "Hey, I was hoping to spend some time with you today!" What is your response and why?

- » "Cool, come shopping with me and we can spend time together while I shop."
- » "Geez, I'm just going to the store. You don't have to spend every moment with me. I will catch you next time."
- » "How about you plan something, and when I get back, we'll do it?"
- » Smirk and walk out the door.

REFLECTIONS Do you know when your partner needs quality time with you? How do you respond when you need time alone?

Partner A

Partner B

First of Many!

Do you know your partner's FIRSTS? After the questions are answered, tally your partner's answers to determine who knew more FIRSTS!

FIRSTS	PARTNER A	PARTNER B
What was your partner's FIRST car?		
What was the name of your partner's FIRST pet?		
What was your partner's FIRST job?		
What did your partner do with their FIRST paycheck?		
What was the FIRST gift you gave your partner?		
When was your partner's FIRST flight on an airplane?		
What was the FIRST state your partner lived in?		
When did your partner FIRST realize they were in love with you?		
Total correct		

The Master of FIRSTS is _____ !

REFLECTIONS Were you both able to answer all the questions? If not, how could you do a better job of sharing your life with each other?

Partner A

Partner B

Date Night Jar!

Date nights help keep your relationship fresh. In this exercise, you'll create a Date Night Jar. Start by labeling colorful Popsicle sticks with a date night idea as indicated by the color key below. Place the sticks inside the mason jar. Randomly draw a stick when you are ready for a new date with your honey! Supplies needed: mason jar, colorful Popsicle sticks (at least two of each color), dark marker.

Popsicle stick colors:

RED: A new restaurant, type of cuisine, or food you've never tried before.

YELLOW: A new adventure. Think of something you haven't done that would get your adrenaline pumping.

BLUE: A date that costs twenty dollars or less.

GREEN: Do something free at home, like a picnic in the living room or "Netflix and chill."

PURPLE: An outdoor date.

> **REFLECTIONS** How often can you commit to using the Date Night Jar?

Partner A

Partner B

Intimacy Through Reading

Intellectual intimacy is the ability to communicate on any level on any topic. There are certain things we can do to create opportunities for intellectual intimacy; one of those is reading together. Below is a list of books that are sure to spark conversation about your relationship. Pick one from the suggestions or find another of your liking. After you read a chapter, discuss what you read and how it can improve your relationship.

Suggestions

The 5 Love Languages: The Secret to Love That Lasts by Gary Chapman

Marriage Rules!: The Hilarious Handbook for Surviving Marriage by Ryan O'Quinn

It's Not Supposed to Be This Way: Finding Unexpected Strength When Disappointments Leave You Shattered by Lysa TerKeurst

I'm Fine and Neither Are You by Camille Pagán

REFLECTIONS This activity may take a couple of weeks to complete. How dedicated can you be to long-term projects that benefit your relationship?

Partner A

Partner B

Top Ten

When we talk about relationships and money, often the focus is on the spending habits of couples. Let's talk about SAVING habits of couples, which can solve some of the spending issues in relationships. List ten new ways that you and your partner can save money. Get creative and be willing to explore all options. An example could be switching out a large cable bill for a less expensive Netflix subscription.

1. _____

2. _____

3. _____

4. _____

5. _____

6. _____

7. _____

8. _____

9. _____

10. _____

REFLECTIONS How easy or difficult is it for you to save money individually? Collectively?

Partner A

Partner B

I Got Your Back

As important as it is for you to grow as a couple, it is equally important for you to grow as individuals. We want our partners to be honest, loving, kind, and supportive, but they don't always know what that looks like. Below, think about ways that your partner can better support you.

Partner A

List three things you are personally working on:

1. _____

2. _____

3. _____

How would you like your mate to support you with the above things?

1. _____

2. _____

3. _____

Partner B

List three things you are personally working on:

1. _____

2. _____

3. _____

How would you like your mate to support you with the above things?

1. _____

2. _____

3. _____

REFLECTIONS How can you better support your partner? What does support look like to you?

Partner A

_____

_____

_____

Partner B

_____

_____

_____

Thank You

Take a few minutes to think of something your partner has done for which you are grateful and then finish this thank-you card.

My Dear _____,

Thank You

for being/doing _____

_____

It makes me feel_____

_____

REFLECTIONS How often do you thank your partner?

Partner A

Partner B

Stick to Me

Sit on the floor with your backs against each other. Divide a pad of sticky notes and write a positive quality about your partner—one quality per sticky note. Don't allow your partner to see your notes. Then, one at a time, put the notes around the house. Once you are both done, walk around the house and read all of the positive things your partner has said about you. Bask in the joy of knowing you are admired by your partner! Supplies needed: a pad of sticky notes, two markers.

REFLECTIONS How did it feel to read the sweet words of your partner? How can you do a better job of complimenting your partner?

Partner A

Partner B

What's on Your Bucket List?

A bucket list is a tally of adventures that a person hopes to complete during their lifetime. What is on your relationship bucket list? What are the big dreams, big goals, big adventures that you hope to accomplish together? Why are these items on your list? What is your timeline for accomplishing them? Together, write about your bucket list and dream big!

_____

_____

_____

_____

_____

_____

REFLECTIONS How did this exercise make you feel?

Partner A

_____

_____

Partner B

_____

_____

Yes or No

Take turns asking each other the questions below. Each question can be answered with only a YES or NO. Be honest!

QUESTION	PARTNER A	PARTNER B
Have you ever fallen going up or down the stairs?		
Have you ever passed gas and blamed it on someone else?		
Have you ever worn the same clothes two days in a row?		
Have you ever worn the same underwear for longer than twenty-four hours?		
Have you ever peed in a swimming pool?		
Would you steal if you were in dire need?		
Would you cheat to win?		
Have you ever been in a fight?		
Have you ever cried because of a movie?		
Have you ever found money and neglected to turn it in?		

REFLECTIONS Were you surprised by any of your partner's answers?

Partner A

Partner B

Box of Feels

Find a shoebox with a lid. Cut a hole in the side of the box that is large enough for a hand to fit through. Gather some random items from around the house. Put an item inside the box, and your partner will guess what it is by sticking their hand inside the hole. They can ask questions and you can offer a clue, if you wish. Take turns going back and forth until both partners have guessed at least five items. The winner is the player who identifies more objects. Supplies needed: shoebox, scissors, random items from around the house.

Below are some suggestions:

- » **Cooked rice or spaghetti**
- » **Seeds from a fresh pumpkin**
- » **A piece of fruit**
- » **Any school supply item**
- » **Jell-O or pudding**

- » **Feathers**
- » **Real and fake flowers**
- » **Toothpaste**
- » **Cereal**

Scores

Partner A _____   **Partner B** _____

REFLECTIONS Sometimes it can be challenging to figure out what our partner is communicating. Can you think of a time when you struggled to understand your partner?

Partner A

Partner B

World's Best

Celebrate your honey! As you peruse the list, think of ways that your partner embodies these qualities and then complete the certificate. Feel free to create your own categories. Hang the certificate next to the bed for a week!

Best Dishwasher	**Best Masseuse**	**Best Thinker**	**Best Kisser**
Best Dancer	**Best Sleeper**	**Best Cooker**	**Best Cuddler**
Best Singer	**Best Vacuumer**	**Best Multitasker**	**Best Driver**

World's Best

This certificate is awarded to

_____

in recognition of

_____

_____   _____
Signature   Date

REFLECTIONS How did it feel to compliment your mate? How did it feel to receive a compliment from your mate?

Partner A

Partner B

Break a Leg

Role-playing is a great way to bring the fun back into your relationship, and this shift in perspective can definitely be exciting. Get creative and use costumes, props, or whatever you have to bring your character to life. Below are a few ideas to get you started. Keep it PG or get a little naughty, but either way, "break a leg" and enjoy!

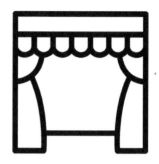

Teacher and Student

Suggested props:

- » Desk
- » Glasses
- » Pencils
- » School uniform
- » Tie
- » Whiteboard

Photographer and Model

Suggested props:

- » Bed
- » Camera
- » Couch
- » Model-style clothing
- » Stairs

Cops and Robbers

Suggested props:

- » Bandana
- » Handcuffs
- » Police costume

Doctor and Patient

Suggested props:

- » Bed
- » Blood pressure band
- » Nurse uniform
- » Scrubs
- » Stethoscope

REFLECTIONS How comfortable were you? Did your partner help you feel relaxed enough to really play?

Partner A

Partner B

Love Letter

In 500 words or fewer, write a love letter to your partner describing how they make your relationship great. Tell your partner why you love being in a relationship with them. After you write it, hide the letter somewhere your partner is sure to find it! Supplies needed: paper, pen.

REFLECTIONS How did it feel to write this letter? How did it feel to receive this letter?

Partner A

Partner B

Get Naked

Being vulnerable means trusting your partner with your heart as you express your innermost thoughts, feelings, and emotions. When you are emotionally vulnerable, it can feel like being emotionally naked. Below are synonyms for the word "vulnerable." Take these words and copy them down onto individual note cards. Then mix the cards up and take turns randomly picking a card and describing how you can be more of that term. Supplies needed: note cards, pen.

- » Accessible
- » Exposed
- » Responsible
- » Ready
- » Sensitive
- » Receptive
- » Open
- » Clear
- » Willing

REFLECTIONS Are you good at "getting naked"?

Partner A

Partner B

Embracing Possibilities

Often, disagreement is viewed as a negative, but every disagreement is rooted in the possibility of agreement. Think about the last time you and your partner struggled to get along. Use the prompts below to think about what you could have done better.

What was the challenge?

_____

_____

During the challenge, what was your perception of the situation?

_____

_____

What could you have done differently to have a better result?

_____

_____

Brainstorm possible solutions to the challenge that you couldn't think of in that moment.

_____

_____

Agree to go through this process the next time you have a challenge!

REFLECTIONS Are you usually good at resolving conflicts? How can you improve?

Partner A

_____

_____

_____

_____

_____

Partner B

_____

_____

_____

_____

_____

Dreaming of a Dream House

What is your mate's idea of a dream home? A sixteen-bedroom mansion in LA? A beautiful ranch-style home in the country? Draw it below and be sure to label all the details you are sure they want!

Partner A Dream Home

Partner B Dream Home

REFLECTIONS Did you know the details of your partner's dream home? How can their vision of a dream home be blended with yours?

Partner A

_____

_____

_____

Partner B

_____

_____

_____

Mixed Fruit

You will each write down a variety of your favorite fruit on separate note cards or small strips of paper, then flip the papers over and mix them up while being careful to keep your piles separate. Take turns pulling from each other's pile. You will explain why that fruit is your favorite and allow your partner to feed it to you and vice versa. Happy eating!

Supplies needed: your favorite fruit; note cards or small strips of paper.

REFLECTIONS How did it feel to feed the fruit to your partner?

Partner A

Partner B

Love Shenanigans

Share the funniest moment you've had together and take a moment to laugh about it all over again!

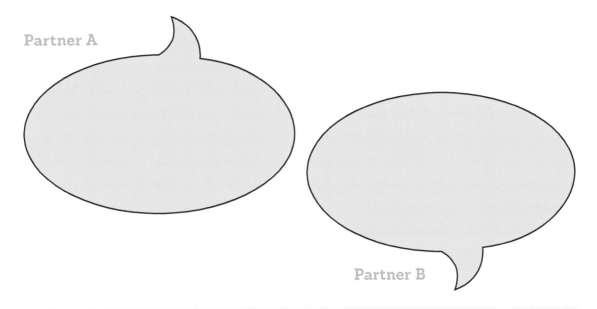

Partner A

Partner B

REFLECTIONS Did you pick the same moment? Are there others you can talk about?

Partner A

Partner B

If Your Love Life Were a Song

Create a romantic mood. Dim the lights, light a candle, or put on some soft music. If you are able, face each other and put this page between you. Hold hands or touch in some way while taking turns answering these questions.

What song best sums up your current love life?

What song best sums up how you felt the first time you ever kissed your partner?

What song best sums up the type of love life you wish you had with your partner?

What song gets you in the mood?

REFLECTIONS Music has the ability to change moods and environments. How can you better incorporate music into your romantic life?

Partner A

_____

_____

Partner B

_____

_____

Relationship Genie

Pretend for a moment that you are sitting in front of the Relationship Genie, who declares, "I am the Relationship Genie! I am here to make your relationship everything you desire it to be! Three wishes will be granted to each of you. What would make your relationship perfect?"

Partner A	Partner B
Wish #1 _____	Wish #1 _____
Wish #2 _____	Wish #2 _____
Wish #3 _____	Wish #3 _____

REFLECTIONS Were you surprised by any of your partner's wishes? Did you agree with the wishes they chose?

Partner A

_____

_____

Partner B

_____

_____

I Need You

Imagine you are traveling somewhere exotic, like to a volcanic island, desert, jungle, or even another planet. Write a short letter to your partner stating the five items you would want them to bring and why you need each item!

Partner A

1. _____

2. _____

3. _____

4. _____

5. _____

Partner B

1. _____

2. _____

3. _____

4. _____

5. _____

REFLECTIONS Were you surprised by the items your partner chose?

Partner A

_____

_____

_____

Partner B

_____

_____

_____

Talk Flirty to Me

Below are some "flirty" words. Use each of their letters to create your own "flirty" words!

S

E

X

T

O

U

C

H

T

I

C

K

L

E

M

O

A

N

C

A

R

E

S

S

K

I

S

S

P

L

E

A

S

U

R

E

P _____

L _____

A _____

Y _____

REFLECTIONS Was it fun coming up with the words? Was it easy or difficult?

Partner A

_____

_____

_____

Partner B

_____

_____

_____

Becoming One

The act of two people becoming one unit can be a challenging process, but conflict is an opportunity to gain a deeper understanding of your partner. If used properly, conflict can transform your relationship in a positive way. Answer the questions below and then discuss the answers with your partner.

Do you try to avoid conflict?

Partner A

Partner B

How does conflict affect each of you differently?

Partner A

Partner B

What does it mean to take a time-out?

Partner A

Partner B

What can be learned from conflict?

Partner A

Partner B

REFLECTIONS How do you manage conflict in other areas of your life?

Partner A

Partner B

Milk Money

Imagine you are at the grocery store with your partner, who has limited funds but wants something from the store and asks you to purchase it.

Do you automatically say yes?

Do you ask how much they can contribute?

Do you ask when they can pay you back?

How do you reply and why?

Think about it and write your responses below.

_____

_____

_____

REFLECTIONS Do you and your partner comingle your funds, or do you keep your money separate?

Partner A

Partner B

_____   _____

_____   _____

Time Hop

Wouldn't it be awesome to have "known" your mate before you "knew" your mate? You have a time machine. Which points in their life would you go back and visit as only an observer?

Partner A

Partner B

REFLECTIONS Why did you pick those points? What do you think of your partner's selections?

Partner A

Partner B

Most Likely

Go through the list and collectively decide who is MOST LIKELY to do each of the below.

ACTIVITY	PARTNER A	PARTNER B
Break out in a dance in public		
Cry over a movie		
Say a prayer before eating a meal		
Sing in the shower		
Have dessert before dinner		
Cheat while playing a board game		
Play in the rain		
Try an exotic food		
Dress up for a Halloween party		
Play a prank on someone		
Go skinny-dipping		
Sing karaoke		
Go skydiving		
Cook a meal at midnight		
	Total	Total

REFLECTIONS Did you struggle with deciding who would do what? Were there things you would both do?

Partner A

Partner B

Verbal GPS: Directions to the Heart

Partner A, fill in the answers to the questions below about your mate, and Partner B will try to guess your answers. Then repeat the process with Partner B answering questions and Partner A guessing.

Partner A, what/who is your partner's BIGGEST . . .

Secret?

Personal goal?

Fear?

Ambition?

Accomplishment?

Celebrity crush?

Academic goal?

Relationship goal?

Annoyance?

Career goal?

Partner B, what/who is your partner's BIGGEST . . .

Secret? _____

Personal goal? _____

Fear? _____

Ambition? _____

Accomplishment? _____

Celebrity crush? _____

Academic goal? _____

Relationship goal? _____

Annoyance? _____

Career goal? _____

REFLECTIONS How did you do? What could help you be more open and vulnerable in your communication?

Partner A

_____

_____

_____

Partner B

_____

_____

_____

Master Daredevil

Take turns reading each "I would rather" statement. One partner answers and the other keeps track of their answers. Then switch roles. The person with the most As is considered the "Master Daredevil"!

I would RATHER . . .

A. Jump out of a plane

B. Watch a movie

If I had superpowers,
I would RATHER . . .

A. Fly

B. Read minds

I would RATHER . . .

A. Ride a roller coaster

B. Ride a Ferris wheel

I would RATHER . . .

A. Eat an octopus

B. Look at one in an aquarium

I would RATHER . . .

A. Swim with dolphins

B. Write a report on dolphins

I would RATHER . . .

A. Go zip-lining

B. Picnic under the trees

I would RATHER . . .

A. Go white water rafting

B. Cruise down a lazy river

I would RATHER . . .

A. Be a pilot

B. Be a passenger on an airplane

I would RATHER . . .

A. Explore an unknown land

B. Watch National Geographic

I would RATHER . . .

A. Solve a mystery case

B. Read a mystery novel

I would RATHER . . .

A. Die trying something new

B. Watch others try new things

I would RATHER . . .

A. Cuddle under the stars

B. Sleep under the stars

Totals

Partner A   As _____   Bs _____

Partner B   As _____   Bs _____

The Award for Master Daredevil goes to _____ !

REFLECTIONS How can you support your partner's "daredevil tendencies"? How can you balance each other out?

Partner A

_____

_____

_____

Partner B

_____

_____

_____

Cuddle Calendar

There are many things that we make reservations for, like nice meals, hotel stays, vacations. Just like making reservations at a restaurant doesn't make it any less of a romantic date, scheduling and preparing for intimacy has its benefits, too!

Pull out your calendars on your phones and schedule four "SEXcapades"! Remember that all four dates must be mutually agreed upon.

In the twenty-four hours leading up to your date, begin to do the following:

1. Send steamy text messages leading up to the main event.
2. Take cute pics and send them to your partner.
3. Pull out your lingerie and cute undergarments.
4. Try new colognes or perfumes and smell brand new for your boo.
5. Bring home a little treat for your partner, like their favorite dessert.

REFLECTIONS How does the planning make this FUN?

Partner A

Partner B

Two Left Feet

Surf the Web and find two songs containing the words "two step." Put on your blindfolds and get ready to get your groove on and cut a rug while not being able to see each other. Use your hands, bodies, and feet to touch each other, BUT SAY NOTHING and have fun moving your bodies to the songs! Your bodies are now your only way to communicate! Supplies needed: two blindfolds; a computer, smartphone, or other device that plays music.

REFLECTIONS How did it feel not being able to speak? Did you still communicate with each other?

Partner A

Partner B

Inspector Gadget

Use the clues below to conquer this couples scavenger hunt!
As you figure out each clue, put a sticky note on that item.
Then count the stickies to see how many you figured out!

1. You open this thing when your stomach is talking to you.

2. This bowl is used to clean your face and teeth.

3. This can be used for a good nap or for "Netflix and chill."

4. This transforms a piece of bread into a crispy masterpiece.

5. You stand and get clean inside this.

6. This rectangle can suck you in with one viewing.

7. We put dirty things inside this and then they come out clean.

8. Things in this drawer are in pairs except when the dryer needs a snack.

9. Lots of things hide out under this dark place.

10. Beans go in and a magical elixir comes out.

11. We put all of the stinky unwanted things in this container.

12. Rubber duckie, you're the one; you make this place so much fun.

13. You go in and out of this, as it is the threshold to your humble abode.

REFLECTIONS Did you struggle to figure out the clues? Did you help each other progress?

Partner A

_____

_____

_____

_____

_____

Partner B

_____

_____

_____

_____

_____

Sugar Pie, Honey Bunch

Did the title make you want to sing and dance? Divide the note cards into two stacks. Each partner will take five minutes to write as many terms of endearment as they can using one note card per term. Then mix them all together.

Partner A randomly chooses two cards. Put those two terms together, and that is the nickname you must call your partner for the next seven days. Partner B will do the same. Supplies needed: note cards, two markers.

REFLECTIONS Did you have nicknames for each other prior to this activity? If not, how does it make you feel to have special names for each other now?

Partner A

Partner B

Sitting Crab

In this exercise, you'll be using two communication strategies:

» **Assertiveness with Compassion,** which is the ability to express yourself honestly and assertively but in a way that allows your mate to receive your words constructively.

» **Heart Listening Skills,** which is the ability to listen with your heart, hear what your mate says, and then be able to paraphrase or repeat it for clarity.

Sit on the ground with your backs to each other, legs bent, and arms linked. You must use both communication strategies to stand up from this position. You cannot unlock your arms or use any furniture or items around you.

> **REFLECTIONS** What strategies did you use to get to the standing position? What was easy about this? What was difficult about this? Could you use these communication strategies in your everyday life?

Partner A

Partner B

Bad Days Go Away, and Don't Come Back Another Day

Everyone has a bad day from time to time, which sometimes affects our mates. Can you think of a time when you had a bad day at work, had a rough day with the kids, or experienced something stressful? Probably several times, right? Now answer the questions below aloud:

1. Have you ever been purposely disagreeable? If so, why?
2. What are the best ways for your partner to engage with you when you are having a "bad day"?
3. Do you know how to soothe yourself and help yourself feel better?
4. What are some healthy ways to deal with "bad days" together as a couple?

> **REFLECTIONS** What are some additional strategies you can implement to help each other deal with the "bad days"?

Partner A

Partner B

Water Play

Dust off your old water guns or buy new ones. Fill them with water and meet your partner outside. Supplies needed: two water guns, water.

Play a variety of water games, including:

» **Hide-and-Seek**
» **Freeze Water Gun Tag**
» **Target Practice**
» **Old-Fashioned Gun Fight**

REFLECTIONS How can you bring more play into your relationship?

Partner A

Partner B

Couple's Journey

During meditation, an individual focuses their mind on a particular object, thought, or activity to achieve a mentally clear and emotionally calm state. Couples meditation builds emotional as well as physical intimacy.

Locate a room in your house that is free of distractions. Light some candles and dim the lights. Sit on the floor in a comfortable position while facing your partner and take each other's hands. If you choose, play some serene music, close your eyes, and try to clear your mind. Meditate on who you are as an individual and then think about who you are in this relationship. Syncing your breathing with your partner's can also create a deep connection. Tuning in to each other on any level is important for understanding and empathy, which lead to love and trust, two of the most powerful cornerstones in any relationship. Start with ten minutes and then, as you feel more comfortable, increase the length of your sessions.

REFLECTIONS Have you ever practiced meditation? How was it today?

Partner A

Partner B

Rest Assured

Quality time with your partner is important, but so is quality time with yourself. We all deserve rest. It's a basic necessity! Below are seven types of rest. Go through the list and determine which kind you need right now. Share that with your partner.

Seven Types of Rest

1. Alone time at home without distraction
2. Doing something unproductive
3. Connecting to art and nature
4. Nap/sleep
5. A break from responsibility
6. Meditation/mindfulness
7. Time away from home

REFLECTIONS How can you support your partner in getting their necessary rest? How can your partner support you?

Partner A

Partner B

Lights, Camera, Action!

People-watching can be a fun activity and a chance to use your imagination and create a story together. You can sit on a park bench, at a local café, or even in a store with a notebook and pen and write down interesting details about the people you see. Consider them potential characters for a novel. When you get home, compare notes. See how similar or different your stories are.

REFLECTIONS Did you and your partner interact much while you were people-watching? Do you think people watch you?

Partner A

_____

_____

_____

Partner B

_____

_____

_____

Trending Perspectives

Below are some hot-button relationship topics. Take turns reading each one and sharing your opinion on it with your partner before a three-minute timer sounds. You each have three minutes to present your perspective before the timer is up! The purpose of this activity is not to agree or disagree with your partner; it's to learn and understand your partner's perspectives.

» Who should be responsible for leading a household? Is it possible to equally lead?

» Should duties be distributed evenly or by a person's strengths?

» Who should manage the inner workings of a household?

» Should financial accounts be separate or joint?

» What's the best way to distribute cooking responsibilities?

» What's the best way to distribute cleaning responsibilities?

REFLECTIONS How difficult is it not to judge your partner as they share? Are you able to respect each other's opinions?

Partner A

Partner B

The Art of Gratitude

A gratitude practice can help you shift your focus from the challenges in your relationship to the positive things that are happening. It is also a great way to build emotional intimacy between you and your partner. Expressing gratitude will help you feel closer emotionally. Take turns answering the questions below out loud to your partner. You can repeat this activity as many times as you like because the reasons for your gratitude should change almost daily.

I am grateful for you because . . .

You made me feel appreciated when . . .

I was happily surprised when you . . .

_____

_____

_____

_____

REFLECTIONS Can you make a daily commitment to have gratitude thoughts regarding your relationship?

Partner A

_____

_____

Partner B

_____

_____

Get to Know Your Mate

Get to know each other by asking and answering the questions below. You are allowed to skip only two questions. Use this exercise over dinner, during your late-night cuddles, or whenever you want to know MORE about each other!

» Tell me about our first kiss.
» What is your favorite external trait about me?
» What is your favorite television show?
» What do you love more than anything?
» What could I not live without?
» What is your favorite internal trait about me?

» What is the one thing no one can do better than you?
» What do you love about our relationship?
» What are your top three turn-ons?
» What is your favorite thing to do on a day off from work?
» What are you most passionate about?

REFLECTIONS Did you learn anything new about your partner?

Partner A

Partner B

Lessons Learned

Life is one of our greatest teachers! If we allowed ourselves to grow and evolve from just "living life," we would be great individuals. Use the prompt below to teach your partner one of your life lessons. I am sure you can think of many things you have learned along the way, but for this activity, just focus on one thing! The listening partner will ask clarifying questions about the particular life lesson that their partner shares. Clarifying something means making it crystal clear! Asking clarifying questions is important in relationships because it helps mates listen with their hearts and not only their ears.

If I knew then what I know now, I would have/would not have . . .

"That's interesting. Tell me more . . ."

"What makes you feel this way?"

Some examples of clarifying questions could be:

"What were your emotions during that time?"

REFLECTIONS Are you accustomed to asking clarifying questions? How do you feel answering clarifying questions?

Partner A

Partner B

Rings of Fun

Pull out your crayons/markers/colored
pencils and get to coloring!

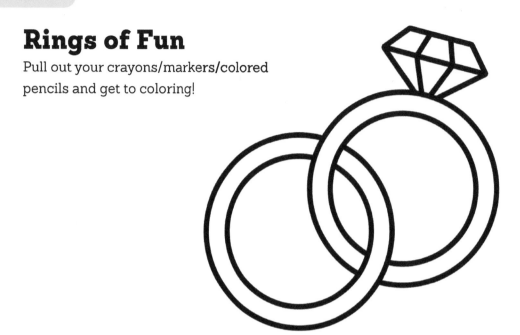

REFLECTIONS Are you currently married? If not, is it a goal for you? If so, why?

Partner A

Partner B

Picture This

Partner A: What is your favorite part of your partner's body? Pull out your inner Picasso and draw it!

Partner B: What is your favorite part of your partner's body? Pull out your inner Picasso and draw it!

REFLECTIONS Why do you love this part of your partner's body? How did it feel to learn what your partner likes about your body?

Partner A

Partner B

Money Talks

Money can be a challenging topic for couples.

Partner A: Inside each square write down your views on each topic and share with your partner.

Debt	Multiple streams of income
Savings	Credit
Entrepreneurship	Taxes

Partner B: Inside each square write down your views on each topic and share with your partner.

Debt	**Multiple streams of income**
Savings	**Credit**
Entrepreneurship	**Taxes**

REFLECTIONS How does this exercise make you feel?

Partner A

_____

_____

_____

_____

_____

Partner B

_____

_____

_____

_____

_____

Easy Like Sunday Morning

Being our partner's helpmate is essential to having a successful relationship. Daily, we should ask the question "How can I make life easier for my partner?" In what ways has your partner made life easier for you? Be explicit and thorough in your explanation. Below are some examples to help get you started.

Ways your partner made things easier for you:

- » Helped with household chores
- » Ran an errand
- » Purchased something that added value to your lives
- » Got rid of something you disliked
- » Noticed when you were overwhelmed, tired, or exhausted, and did something to help you feel better

Partner A

Partner B

REFLECTIONS Offer one way you can make your partner's life easier.

Partner A

Partner B

REFLECTIONS Share one way your partner can make your life easier.

Partner A

Partner B

Let's Talk About It

It's the first of the month, and the mortgage/rent is your financial responsibility, but you don't have enough to cover the payment. Do you . . .

Partner A

1. Explain the situation to your partner and figure out how to resolve it together?
2. Get a loan from a friend or credit card cash advance and then tell your mate you resolved the issue?
3. Resolve the issue by yourself and never inform your partner?

Partner B

1. Explain the situation to your partner and figure out how to resolve it together?
2. Get a loan from a friend or credit card cash advance and then tell your mate you resolved the issue?
3. Resolve the issue by yourself and never inform your partner?

REFLECTIONS What do you think of your mate's response?

Partner A

Partner B

Mix It Up to Keep It Up

It is tempting to want your partner to think the way you do, but you are different people, which means you have different points of view. Studies of human behavior have noted that people make decisions based on thinking or feelings. Those making decisions based on *feelings* use their value systems and what they perceive as right or wrong. Those making decisions based on *thinking* use rational, impartial, and logical thoughts.

Partner A

Who is primarily the thinker and who is primarily the feeler in your relationship?

Why do you feel your answer is accurate?

What proof do you have?

How have you both mastered the art of compromise considering the differences in your personalities?

Partner A

Partner B

Who is primarily the thinker and who is primarily the feeler in your relationship?

Why do you feel your answer is accurate?

What proof do you have?

How have you both mastered the art of compromise considering the differences in your personalities?

Partner B

_____

_____

_____

_____

_____

_____

REFLECTIONS Compromise is the art of relationships. Discuss whether or not you both agree on the labels you provided above.

Co-parenting Calendar

You and your partner are making time to grow your relationship, which is fantastic. But it is important to keep in mind the relationship you have with your children as well.

Use these two monthly calendars to schedule date nights with your family. Be sure to include:

» **Two dates a month with each child. (The dates can be as simple as board game night in the living room.)**
» **Two dates a month as an entire family.**
» **At least two dates a month with only your partner.**

SUN	MON	TUE	WED	THU	FRI	SAT

SUN	MON	TUE	WED	THU	FRI	SAT

REFLECTIONS Was it difficult negotiating the dates? Will you make this calendar a regular habit?

Partner A

Partner B

Date with a Purpose

Dating gives us a chance to have fun, laugh, and enjoy each other! Use the dating-related clues below to complete the crossword puzzle!

Across

2. We spend our childhood doing this but forget it's still a part of our adulthood.

3. Singing with video assistance.

5. Sweet treat for the perfect date night.

7. Moving rhythmically, typically to music.

9. Ten pins and one ball equal a STRIKE of a date night!

10. Sexy, short, or long. She will bring it to life for your date night.

12. What you feel when you spend time with your partner.

14. Right foot, left foot, glide. Can be done on ice or wood.

16. They can be red or white, dry or sweet.

17. A form of walking.

Down

1. Hop on the swings here and push your partner while enjoying their laughter.

4. Get served. Eat well. Enjoy the conversation.

6. The process of creating artistic visuals.

8. Used for your sipping pleasure.

11. Mountains, hills, or trails. It's a great way to get a view.

13. Big screens, blockbusters. The most common date activity.

15. This goes around your neck like a choker but makes you look like a classic man.

REFLECTIONS How did it feel to work together on this puzzle? Did it bring back any memories?

Partner A

Partner B

Sharing Time Together

Spending time together is probably one of the most important things you can do as a couple. Pull out your local newspaper or go online to discover events going on in your city, town, and state. Look for things that you would both consider fun. Come up with ten events you would like to do TOGETHER over the next year! It could be attending a local play or joining an adult softball team. As long as the activity is something you can enjoy together, it goes on the list!

1. _____
2. _____
3. _____
4. _____
5. _____

6. _____
7. _____
8. _____
9. _____
10. _____

REFLECTIONS Are you content with the amount of time you currently spend together?

Partner A

Partner B

Discuss ways you can create more time for each other.

Smart Music

Take a couple of hours to listen to music on whatever music applications you use. Every time you hear a song that reminds you of your partner, jot it down on a sheet of paper or note it in your phone. They can be songs that make you laugh, cry, or dance, as long as they remind you of your partner. Then create a playlist for your honey of all the songs that remind you of them. Explain to your partner why each song made you think of them. Don't forget to give the playlist a name! Supplies needed: a computer, smartphone, or other device that plays music.

REFLECTIONS Did any of the songs you selected come from a particular day or special moment?

Partner A

Partner B

Our Monthly Budget

In order to meet your financial goals, you and your partner will need to assess your current situation. Choose a quiet time to sit down and create a monthly budget. You will need financial documents and records, such as copies of your pay stubs, monthly bills, receipts, etc. This document will change over time, so consider revisiting it often.

INCOME	BUDGET	ACTUAL	DIFFERENCE
Partner A salary (after tax)			
Partner B salary (after tax)			
Investments			
Other Income			
Total			

EXPENSES	AMOUNT	ACTUAL	DIFFERENCE
Insurance			
Groceries			
Mortgage/rent			
Gas			
Dining out			
Laundry & personal care			
Car loan			
Utilities			
Clothing			
Day care			
Medical/dental			
Household repairs			

EXPENSES	AMOUNT	ACTUAL	DIFFERENCE
Savings accounts			
Cell phone bill			
Personal allowance			
Total			

TOTALS	BUDGET	ACTUAL	DIFFERENCE
Monthly income			
Monthly expenses			

Notes

REFLECTIONS Was it easy to be honest about your finances? How often can you commit to sitting down together and reviewing and/or editing this budget?

Partner A

Partner B

Maze Craze!

One partner wears a blindfold while the other partner attempts to guide them through the maze using only their words. Have fun with this and remember that getting through the maze perfectly isn't the goal, but communicating properly is! Supplies needed: blindfold, pen.

Partner A

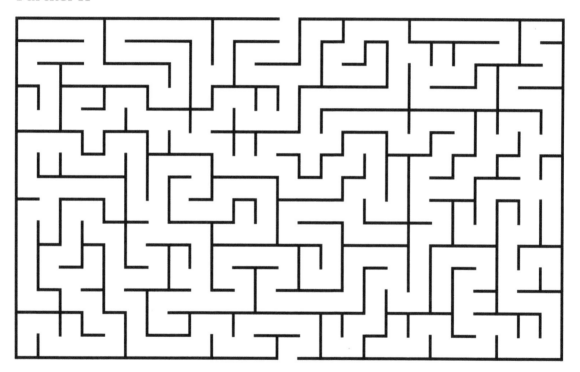

Partner B

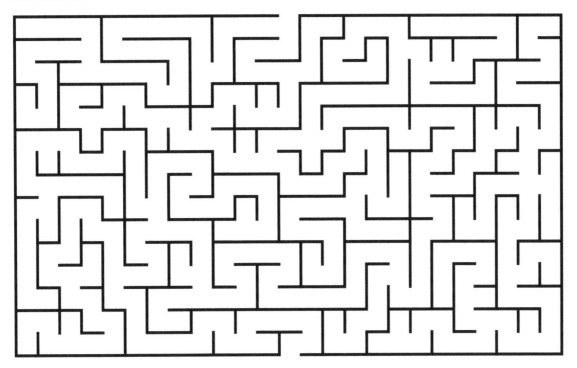

REFLECTIONS How did you do? Who gave better directions? Who listened better?

Partner A

Partner B

I Love You 3,000

You love your partner for a million reasons. Take an opportunity to think about all the wonderful traits that make your partner your personal superhero and then draw them as one!

Partner A

Partner B

REFLECTIONS What are your favorite traits of your partner? What is their kryptonite?

Partner A

_____

_____

_____

_____

_____

Partner B

_____

_____

_____

_____

_____

Dare to Be Romantic

Below is a list of romantic dares to spice up your relationship! Take turns completing the dares until your heart is content or racing! ;-)

1. Kiss your partner ten times anywhere on their body.
2. Seduce your partner without touching them.
3. Write your name on your partner's body using your fingers.
4. Pick your favorite slow song and dance for your partner.
5. Read a romantic poem to your partner.
6. Take your partner for a long car ride at midnight.
7. Tell your partner you love them in three different ways.
8. Take a shower with your partner.
9. Put together a romantic picnic under the stars.
10. Give your partner a massage.
11. Show your partner a romantic gesture in public.
12. Treat your partner like a king/ queen for the night and cater to their every need.
13. Wear something sexy while eating breakfast or dinner at home.
14. Allow your partner to dress you for a date.

REFLECTIONS Which was the most exciting dare? The most challenging? Which will you do again?

Partner A

Partner B

Kiss-Off

Good kissing is an art that should be practiced often. Little kisses lead to more meaningful ones, and more kisses lead to increased intimacy. While Partner A puts on some lipstick— preferably a deep color that will show up well on your partner's skin—Partner B will look for a song with the word "kiss" in it. Partner A will get ready to cover them in kisses while Partner B presses "play" and prepares to be kissed! Partner A will kiss their mate all over their face for the next sixty seconds.

At the end of the sixty seconds, count the number of lipstick marks on Partner B's face. Each mark equals a minute, and each minute represents the amount of time you owe your partner a massage. Bonus! You have created intimacy through music and your lips, and next you will create it with your hands. Supplies needed: a dark-colored lipstick; something to listen to music on, like a smartphone.

REFLECTIONS Do you enjoy kissing? What does intimacy look like in your relationship?

Partner A

Partner B

Rules of Engagement

Even after many years of marriage, most couples still fight, but there is a method to the madness! The secret is that there is "fighting fair" and "fighting unfair." When a couple learns to fight fair, the conflict usually brings them closer versus pulling them apart. What exactly does it mean to fight fair? So glad you asked! Fairness means justice and acting morally when conflict arises. So, ground rules are in order, and you have to agree to the rules BEFORE conflict happens.

Create the Fight Fair Rules for your relationship. See a few examples below to get you started. Remember that the quality of your "fair fighting" depends on your ability to be honest and creative with your rules!

1. Don't aim to belittle or berate each other. Remember that your purpose is to come to an understanding and not to hurt each other with cheap shots and insults.

2. Stick to the subject. When a number of issues seem to be arising, address them one at a time. If you have not resolved past issues, put them on a current or future agenda, but don't try to resolve multiple issues in one conversation.

3. _____

4. _____

5. _____

6. _____

7. _____

8. _____

9. _____

10. _____

REFLECTIONS Which of these rules will be the most difficult for you to follow?

Partner A

_____

_____

_____

_____

Partner B

_____

_____

_____

_____

The Power of Criticism

It is very important that we accept our partners for who they are, especially when it comes to those traits they can't change. However, it's equally important that couples be able to provide each other with constructive criticism when necessary. Who better to provide constructive criticism than the person you love who has your best interests at heart? Constructive criticism allows us to grow, change, and evolve—if we allow it!

Write down one thing about your partner that you think they can improve and how you can help them do so.

Partner A

_____

_____

_____

_____

Partner B

_____

_____

_____

_____

REFLECTIONS What are your reservations about giving your partner feedback?
How do you feel about receiving constructive criticism?

Partner A

Partner B

Sit Up or Pull Up

Exercise is necessary for our personal health, so why not make it necessary for your relationship health? Exercising together has many benefits, including accountability, encouragement, motivation, and more opportunities to spend time together. Try some of the exercises below or make up your own. It is important to allow your partner to work out on their level. Make sure you stretch first!

» Walking/jogging: Create small goals along the way. For example, if you are walking or jogging in your neighborhood, plan to stop at the stop signs for small talk and to congratulate each other.

» Sit-ups: One partner holds the other partner's legs and does five to ten sit-ups at a time before switching positions. Give each other a high five every time you switch places.

» Jumping jacks: Cheer each other along the way as you do your jumping jacks at the same pace.

» Squats: Face each other and maintain eye contact as you go up and down.

» Ball toss: Stand in front of each other with a ball. Shuffle four steps to the left and right as you toss the ball between the two of you.

After your workout, give each other a quick massage.

REFLECTIONS Have you ever worked out together? Is this an activity that you would repeat?

Partner A

_____

_____

_____

_____

_____

Partner B

_____

_____

_____

_____

_____

I'm Sorry

We're human, so of course we'll do something to offend our partner on occasion. But how good are we at apologizing when we do? Think about a time when you offended your partner in a small or big way. Perhaps you both have moved on from the offense, even though you never apologized. Take a moment to write an apology letter to your partner. Be sure to include the offense, why it happened, an acknowledgment of how you may have made your partner feel, and one way you can rectify the situation. Apologies require us to let down our pride and help us be more vulnerable with our partners. There is a sheet for both partners.

Partner A

Dear _____ ,

_____

_____

_____

_____

_____

_____

_____

Partner B

Dear _____ ,

_____

_____

_____

_____

_____

_____

_____

REFLECTIONS How difficult is it for you to apologize to your partner?

Partner A

_____

_____

_____

Partner B

_____

_____

_____

Righty Tighty, Lefty Loosey

Are you a righty or a lefty? Use your nondominant hand to write your partner's name. Whoever does it better wins!

REFLECTIONS Who won the competition? Is it easy or difficult to compete against someone you love?

Partner A

Partner B

List of Last

Based on the answers below, you'll both discover how much attention you've been paying to your partner's actions, behaviors, words, and thoughts.

Partner A

1. When was your partner's last haircut?
2. What was the last meal your partner ate?
3. What was the last meal your partner prepared?
4. When was the last time your partner went to the gas station?
5. What color shoes did your partner have on last?
6. What was the last goal your partner accomplished?
7. When was your partner's last trip to the doctor?
8. What was the last perfume your partner purchased?
9. When was your partner's last day off?
10. What was your partner's last pet?
11. What were your partner's last words to you?
12. When was the last time your partner became ill?
13. When was the last time your partner cried?
14. What was the last book your partner read?
15. When did your partner last exercise?
16. When was your last physical connection with your partner?
17. What was your partner's last adult beverage?
18. Whom did your partner last text?
19. If the world were ending, what would be your partner's last meal?
20. What was the last movie your partner saw at the theater?

Partner B

1. When was your partner's last haircut?
2. What was the last meal your partner ate?
3. What was the last meal your partner prepared?
4. When was the last time your partner went to the gas station?
5. What color shoes did your partner have on last?
6. What was the last goal your partner accomplished?
7. When was your partner's last trip to the doctor?
8. What was the last perfume your partner purchased?
9. When was your partner's last day off?
10. What was your partner's last pet?
11. What were your partner's last words to you?
12. When was the last time your partner became ill?
13. When was the last time your partner cried?
14. What was the last book your partner read?
15. When did your partner last exercise?
16. When was your last physical connection with your partner?
17. What was your partner's last adult beverage?
18. Whom did your partner last text?
19. If the world were ending, what would be your partner's last meal?
20. What was the last movie your partner saw at the theater?

REFLECTIONS How much attention do you pay to your partner? Were these questions easy or difficult to answer?

Partner A

_____

_____

_____

_____

Partner B

_____

_____

_____

_____

I Agree, I Disagree

What do you think it takes to have a successful relationship? Below is a list of several statements, assumptions, and clichés about successful relationships. Go through each and determine if you individually AGREE or DISAGREE. This activity is less about being right or wrong and more about having open and honest dialogue about each statement.

Partner A

Traits of successful relationships:

- » Have very few disagreements
- » Share responsibilities
- » Engage in lots of sexual or intimate activities
- » Communicate about everything
- » Have joint bank accounts
- » Only spend time together, because they don't need friends since they have each other
- » Agree on the ways in which to raise children
- » Always keep a secret stash of cash
- » Are each other's best friends
- » Make their relationship a priority
- » Set healthy boundaries
- » Don't share fears so that they don't bring negativity into the relationship
- » Put their kids first and the relationship afterward

Partner B

Traits of successful relationships:

- » Have very few disagreements
- » Share responsibilities
- » Engage in lots of sexual or intimate activities
- » Communicate about everything
- » Have joint bank accounts
- » Only spend time together, because they don't need friends since they have each other
- » Agree on the ways in which to raise children
- » Always keep a secret stash of cash
- » Are each other's best friends
- » Make their relationship a priority
- » Set healthy boundaries
- » Don't share fears so that they don't bring negativity into the relationship
- » Put their kids first and the relationship afterward

REFLECTIONS Did any of your partner's answers surprise you? What did you learn about your partner?

Partner A

Partner B

_____

_____

_____

State Your Opinion

Put on your competitive cap and see who can label the states on this map of the United States faster! First, one partner races around the map while the other partner times them, then vice versa. The game doesn't end until you have labeled all states or given up!

Partner A Time _____

Partner B Time

REFLECTIONS How did you do? Are you as traveled as you want to be?

Partner A

Partner B

Check Points

Having "check points"—times when you check in with your partner with vulnerability and honesty—can keep you and your partner on track to reach your goals. At least once a month, grade each other (from A to F) on the following items and try to push through the uncomfortable questions. Without this kind of check-in, it is easy to let issues fester and develop resentments.

Partner A grades Partner B

1. Being a partner
2. Sharing responsibilities
3. Getting enough alone time
4. Spending enough time together
5. Being helpful
6. Doing better on issues previously discussed
7. Speaking respectfully
8. Making me feel heard
9. Making me feel understood
10. Forgiving

Partner B grades Partner A

1. Being a partner
2. Sharing responsibilities
3. Getting enough alone time
4. Spending enough time together
5. Being helpful
6. Doing better on issues previously discussed
7. Speaking respectfully
8. Making me feel heard
9. Making me feel understood
10. Forgiving

REFLECTIONS Can you commit to asking and answering these questions monthly? Are you vulnerable enough to be honest with your answers?

Partner A

Partner B

Name That Tune!

Hum your favorite tunes and see if your honey can guess them!
Tally the score and reward the winner!

Partner A _____

Partner B _____

> **REFLECTIONS** Who was quicker? Who has the better ear?

Partner A

_____

_____

Partner B

_____

_____

Truth or Dare: Couples Edition

Take turns rolling the die. Even numbers are TRUTHS and odd numbers are DARES. Feel free to add your own! Supplies needed: one die.

Truths

- » Describe your favorite clothing style.
- » Have you ever taken an inappropriate selfie?
- » What kind of food turns you on?
- » What is a household chore you hate to do?

Dares

- » Pretend the broom is a guitar and stream a stage-worthy performance on the Internet.
- » Hop like a frog around the house for sixty seconds.
- » Serenade your partner.
- » Give your partner a sexy dance.

REFLECTIONS What did you learn about your partner? Which dare was most exciting?

Partner A

Partner B

Love Jones

Poetry is the lover's language. Poetry can be extremely romantic and become a creative way to express your love for your honey! Today you will write some love poetry but with a twist! Make sure that it rhymes and expresses the sentiments of your heart. Here is the kicker: You may NOT use the words "love," "like," or "heart."

Go Partner A!

Go Partner B!

How can you infuse poetry into your intimacy on a monthly basis?

Partner A

Partner B

Brainteasers

Read these brainteasers aloud and see who can answer them first.

1. If you take off my skin, I won't cry, but you will! What am I?

   Answer:

2. Gilles, Robert, and Michael are married to Louise, Carole, and Lily. Who are the couples? (Hints: Louise's sister is married to Michael. Gilles has never met Lily, who is an only child.)

   Answer:

3. What's beautiful and natural but gets long and prickly if it isn't trimmed regularly?

   Answer:

4. Imagine you're in a room that is filling with water. There are no windows or doors. How do you get out?

   Answer:

5. I'm present at every meal, but I never get eaten. What am I?

   Answer:

6. What do you call it when your parachute doesn't open?

   Answer:

7. What can you catch but not throw?

   Answer:

8. Which five-letter word becomes shorter when you add two letters to it?

   Answer:

9. Mr. Blue lives in the blue house, Mr. Yellow lives in the yellow house, and Mr. Black lives in the black house. Who lives in the white house?

   Answer:

10. What does a man do only once in his lifetime but women do once a year after age twenty-nine?

    Answer:

11. What's white, minty, and better to spit than to swallow?

    Answer:

12. What starts off as dry and hard but becomes soft and wet after you use it?

    Answer:

13. What has hands but can't clap?

    Answer:

REFLECTIONS Did any of the questions stump you? Did you help each other figure them out?

Partner A

_____

_____

_____

_____

Partner B

_____

_____

_____

_____

Report Card

Children can be our greatest joy, and being a parent is an opportunity to create, shape, and mold a human. Have an open discussion about your children with your partner and use this sheet to jot down your answers. Be honest with your mate. Be realistic as well.

Partner A

What are your favorite internal traits about your children?

What are your favorite external traits about your children?

What traits did they take from you and/or your partner?

What are your short-term goals for your children?

What are your long-term goals for your children?

What is your greatest fear for your children?

What is a challenge that you will have to overcome as a parent in order to raise your children?

What is your child's favorite subject in school, and how does that correlate with their career goals?

After high school, do you want your children to attend college, take a gap year, go into the military, go right into work, or just explore the world before they make any decisions?

Partner B

What are your favorite internal traits about your children?

What are your favorite external traits about your children?

What traits did they take from you and/or your partner?

What are your short-term goals for your children?

What are your long-term goals for your children?

What is your greatest fear for your children?

What is a challenge that you will have to overcome as a parent in order to raise your children?

What is your child's favorite subject in school, and how does that correlate with their career goals?

After high school, do you want your children to attend college, take a gap year, go into the military, go right into work, or just explore the world before they make any decisions?

REFLECTIONS Being a parent can be rewarding and overwhelming. How has it been for you?

Partner A

Partner B

Tell a Time When . . .

This activity will jog your memory and reveal things about yourself and your partner. Take turns asking and answering these prompts out loud to each other.

1. You laughed so hard that your belly hurt . . .

2. You cried watching a movie . . .

3. You belted out your favorite song in the shower . . .

4. You felt proud of yourself . . .

5. You felt proud of your partner . . .

6. You received a reward (and explain how you felt afterward) . . .

7. You rewarded yourself . . .

8. You felt loved unconditionally . . .

9. You saved money to buy something special . . .

10. You went to a restaurant and ate alone . . .

11. You went on a date that had you smiling for twenty-four hours . . .

12. You ate something exotic . . .

13. You took a trip to the beach . . .

14. You took a trip to the mountains . . .

15. You wrote a love note . . .

16. You received a love note . . .

REFLECTIONS What did you learn about your partner?

Partner A

_____

_____

_____

_____

_____

Partner B

_____

_____

_____

_____

_____

Romantic Résumé

Think about all of your partner's most attractive qualities. What would you put on their romantic résumé? Start with the prompts below:

Partner A about Partner B

First and last name:

_____

AKA (the term of endearment you call them):

_____

Draw a picture of your partner.

```




```

Describe your partner in three sentences.

If your partner had a website, what would it be called?

What are they best at doing around the house?

What is your favorite thing that they do romantically?

What are the ways your partner makes you laugh?

What are their strengths?

How have they evolved throughout your relationship?

First and last name:

_____

AKA (the term of endearment you call them):

_____

Draw a picture of your partner.

```
┌─────────────────────────────────────────────┐
│                                               │
│                                               │
│                                               │
│                                               │
│                                               │
│                                               │
│                                               │
│                                               │
│                                               │
│                                               │
└─────────────────────────────────────────────┘
```

Describe your partner in three sentences.

_____

_____

_____

If your partner had a website, what would it be called?

What are they best at doing around the house?

What is your favorite thing that they do romantically?

What are the ways your partner makes you laugh?

What are their strengths?

How have they evolved throughout your relationship?

REFLECTIONS How did it feel to read the kind things your partner wrote about you?

Partner A

Partner B

My Relationship Review

Imagine your relationship is a book. Would it be a romance? A thriller?
A fairy tale? Answer the questions below:

Partner A name:
Partner B name:
Title of your book:
Date your book was published:
What is the story line?
Who are the main characters? The heroes? The villains?
What obstacles must the hero(es) overcome?
What is your favorite part of the book?
What are the new chapters that you plan to write?

REFLECTIONS Which parts of your book do you like best? How can you add more excitement to your book?

Partner A

_____

_____

_____

_____

Partner B

_____

_____

_____

_____

ANSWER KEY

AH-MAZING FUN!

BABIES 'N' THINGS

Across

6. At the beginning, your baby will see them often, and after a while, your baby will only see them annually: DOCTORS

8. What your child does when they want your attention, or are hungry, sleepy, sick, and everything in between: CRY

9. After being up with a newborn for seven consecutive nights, you feel: SLEEPY

11. After every meal, put your nose plug on and grab your gloves because there is bound to be some: POOP

12. Rattle, stuffed animals, bears, blocks: TOYS

13. Sometimes it has two wheels or four wheels, and it is a lifesaver in public: STROLLER

15. Your lips just can't help it! You probably plant these on your little one daily: KISSES

Down

1. What a baby does after you give them a bottle and then attempt to play with them: VOMIT

2. Your favorite thing to do with your new little bundle of joy: CUDDLE

3. An intimate connection between Mommy and baby: NURSING

4. They may be a teenager, but they love your child(ren) as their own: BABYSITTER

5. There is nothing sweeter than coming home from work and getting to be _____ with your child(ren): SILLY

7. Children love to explore and are _____ about the world: CURIOUS

10. What children want to do as soon as your eyes close for a nap: PLAY

14. What we feel for our children the second they are born: LOVE

BABIES 'N' THINGS

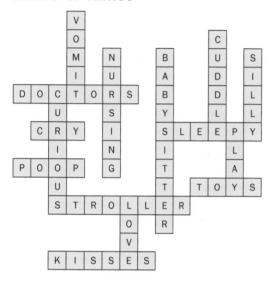

BRAINTEASERS

If you take off my skin, I won't cry, but you will! What am I?

Answer: Onion.

Gilles, Robert, and Michael are married to Louise, Carole, and Lily. Who are the couples?

Hints: Louise's sister is married to Michael. Gilles has never met Lily, who is an only child.

Answer: Louise and Gilles. Carole and Michael. Lily and Robert.

What's beautiful and natural but gets long and prickly if it isn't trimmed regularly?

Answer: Grass.

Imagine you're in a room that is filling with water. There are no windows or doors. How do you get out?

Answer: Stop imagining.

I'm present at every meal, but I never get eaten. What am I?

Answer: Plate.

What do you call it when your parachute doesn't open?

Answer: Jumping to a conclusion.

What can you catch but not throw?

Answer: A cold.

Which five-letter word becomes shorter when you add two letters to it?

Answer: Short.

Mr. Blue lives in the blue house, Mr. Yellow lives in the yellow house, and Mr. Black lives in the black house. Who lives in the white house?

Answer: The president.

What does a man do only once in his lifetime but women do once a year after age twenty-nine?

Answer: Turn thirty.

What's white, minty, and better to spit than to swallow?

Answer: Toothpaste.

What starts off as dry and hard but becomes soft and wet after you use it?

Answer: Sponge.

What has hands but can't clap?

Answer: A clock.

COMPATIBILITY MIX-UP

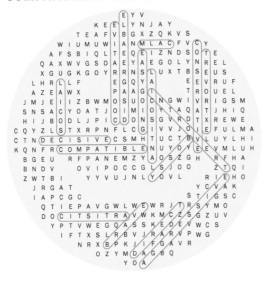

KISS 'N' TELL

DATE WITH A PURPOSE

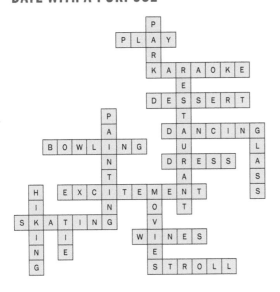

LET'S GET THROUGH IT!

1. iamensteeDrg — Disagreement
2. eevsoRl — Resolve
3. tGrhwo — Growth
4. nitasDt — Distant
5. eteegmArn — Agreement
6. ehpztaEmi — Emphasize
7. nlCfcoti — Conflict
8. giaTnkl — Talking
9. elginlY — Yelling
10. oCep — Cope
11. eExrolp — Explore
12. evLo — Love
13. rreTiggs — Triggers
14. emrmCsiopo — Compromise

15. rgoenI   Ignore
16. ncptePoeri   Perception
17. iooEtnsm   Emotions
18. oiuRleston   Resolution
19. lpvEisxoe   Explosive
20. nLitngise   Listening

MATCH UP YOUR RESOLUTION
1. b; 2. e; 3. j; 4. a; 5. i; 6. g; 7. c; 8. f; 9. d; 10. h

MAZE CRAZE!

MONEY MANAGEMENT IS KING!
1. ignninfac   financing
2. ahsc   cash
3. niceom   income
4. rsi   IRS
5. retdic   credit
6. nile   lien
7. tssea   asset
8. lctaaip   capital
9. noal   loan
10. ecefarticit fo sopdiet   certificate of deposit
11. ari   IRA
12. eepesxns   expenses
13. aduti   audit
14. bedt   debt
15. onaccut   account
16. uebdtg   budget
17. dnob   bond
18. sach dvneaac   cash advance
19. ilne fo iretcd   line of credit
20. etla eef   late fee
21. ddeidniv   dividend
22. entsnteivms   investments
23. yemon   money
24. sasvgin   savings
25. kcotss   stocks
26. rmrteiente   retirement
27. galso   goals

ABOUT THE AUTHOR

Patrice Webb Bush is the founder and CEO of It Takes 2 Marriage Coaching, which has as its mission to strengthen families through couples coaching, destination marriage retreats, workshops, and support groups. It Takes 2 has served more than 650 couples across thirty-four US states. From 2014 to 2016, Patrice hosted the *Marriage Matters* radio show, which had more than 8,000 listeners. Patrice is an executive trainer and a public speaker. She has appeared on Fox News and several radio shows across the country, and has been published in *Charlotte Parent* magazine. You can reach Patrice via social media at the following:

WEBSITE *https://ittakes2marriagecoaching.com*
FACEBOOK *https://www.facebook.com/ItTakes2MarriageCoaching*
INSTAGRAM *@ittakes2marriagecoaching*

CPSIA information can be obtained
at www.ICGtesting.com
Printed in the USA
JSHW010320231119
2524JS00004B/4